Deer at the Red Sea

Stubborn, the sunset insisted on staying
In the Red Sea at night, when they first
Come to the palace of water — the innocent-pink,
Noble deer, to still their thirst.

They leave their silk shadows on the shore.
With violin faces, they lick the rings of gold
In the Red Sea. And there it happens,
Their betrothal with silence — lo and behold!

Finished — they flee. Pink spots
Enliven the sand. But the sunset deer,
Moaning, remain in the water, and lick
The silence of those who will no more appear.

                          Abraham Sutzkever

Dedication

In every era, God calls His royal children to step up and serve as:

- history-makers and culture-changers
- cupbearers and kingmakers
- gatekeepers and judges
- sentinels and watchmen
- mentors and benefactors
- bridge-builders and navigators
- armour-bearers and gamechangers

As once He called Adam to be His 'shomer'
— a guardian, protector and keeper of the earth —
so too He summons us to that same privilege.
To be His 'shomer', His royal keeper,
charged with the healing of history.
To follow in the footsteps of Jesus and,
through the most ordinary everyday activities,
mend the world.

To you,
invited to be a 'shomer' of the Most High,
may Jesus show you
how to fulfil your calling.

Anne Hamilton
Seventeen Mile Rocks
Passover, 2020

Contents

1	*Deer at the Red Sea*
5	Introduction
6	*The Garden*
9	**Deer at the Dawning of the Day**
22	Discussion Questions
24	Prayer
30	*Emmaus*
32	**The Road**
62	Notes about the healing of Emmaus's history
66	Discussion Questions
67	Prayer
68	Acknowledgments and Attributions
70	*Love's Redeeming Work is Done*

Introduction

In his absorbing cultural analysis, *Strange Days*, Mark Sayers reflects on the modern concept of 'places' and 'non-places'. Homes and other locations that engender a sense of belonging — such as a workplace, a friend's house, a church — are 'places'. Airports, hotels, highways are examples of 'non-places'.

The 'non-place', unlike the 'place', does not tell us who we are. 'Places' foster a strong sense of history, relationship and identity. 'Non-places' deconstruct these roots of family and tradition in the interests of globalisation. The relentless drive towards a world without boundaries fractures our sense of the sacred, leaving us dislocated and displaced.

The books in this series are about very specific 'places'. There is nothing interchangeable about the location in any story. What Jesus did at Shechem was so focussed on the history unique to that locality it would not have made sense in Galilee. His proclamation at Caesarea Philippi could have been uttered in Jerusalem, but He would not have been speaking to the surrounding land itself.

This volume contains one essay and one narrative re-telling of events concerning the Resurrection. In each case, 'place' is absolutely crucial. In a world busy erasing borders of every imaginable kind, forcing us to be 'spiritually placeless because the boundaries of locations sacred and pure … are punctured, crossed or abused,'* Jesus shows us the importance of intentionality with regard to 'place'.

The healing of history is never formulaic or general; it's always a bespoke solution, lovingly crafted to specific hurts and harms. May your heart lift in praise as you read the following pages. May you be blessed with wonder at how Jesus stitched together the torn tapestry of time merely by walking the Emmaus road, and through a simple conversation with a woman in a garden.

The Jewish people of today have a word for a divinely orchestrated sudden reversal: 've'nahafochu', *And everything was turned upside down.*

Whatever healing you need today in your own history or place, may you too know the 've'nahafochu' of God.

Anne Hamilton
Seventeen Mile Rocks
Passover, 2020

---

* Mark Sayers, *Strange Days: Life in the Spirit in a Time of Upheaval*, Moody Publishers 2017

"Make haste, my beloved, and be like a gazelle
or a young stag upon the mountains of spices."

— Song of Solomon 8:14 KJV —

THE GARDEN

The Lord God called out to the man
and asked, "Where are you?"

Genesis 3:9 CEV

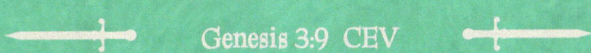

John 20:15 GWT

Mary thought it was the gardener speaking to her.
So she said to Him, "Sir, if you carried Him away,
tell me where you have put Him ..."

Deer at the Dawning of the Day

*O let me rise
As larks, harmoniously,
And sing this day thy victories ...*

George Herbert, *Easter Wings*

> The title, *Deer at the Dawning of the Day*, is inspired by the name of the tune given in the musical notation at the heading of Psalm 22. The wording comes from the Passion Translation.

Early one Sunday morning, in the shadowy coolness of a garden, a grieving woman approached a man she thought was a gardener. Her words pulse with ancient echoes — they gather in prophecy and heresy, and bind them together with history long gone and yet to come. Simple and unpremeditated, Mary Magdalene's words open up the deathly wounds of the past for Jesus to heal.

'They have taken my Lord away ... and I don't know where they have put Him.'[1]

Basically, she's saying: 'Where is the Lord?' That's the aching question in her heart. Her words, though unremarkable and perfectly ordinary on the surface, in fact hark back to another garden — at the dawn of history. In Eden, in the cool of the day, God the gardener came looking for mankind. 'Where are you?' He asked.

> 1.
> John 20:13 NIV

In Jerusalem, in the cool of the day, the opposite happened. A representative of mankind came into a garden, looking for God. 'Where is He?' she asked.

At that moment, Jesus and Mary were reversing Eden. The simplicity of their meeting belies its significance. God's words back in Eden as He called to Adam indicate there had been a severing of the oneness between humanity and Himself. 'Where are you?' is a question that shows union has been ruptured.

However the scene in the garden outside the tomb shows that the breach was not irreversible. Covenantal oneness had been made possible once more.

This reversal was only the beginning. The short dialogue between Mary and Jesus captures immeasurably more out of the pages of history than the fall of humanity in Eden. Mary was not simply a representative of mankind in a generic sense: her inspired words encode specialised meaning for Jews and Gentiles as well as Samaritans.

There are not many names that are devised around questions. One of them is Michael, meaning *who is like God?* Another is Jezebel,

Mary stood outside the tomb weeping.
John 20:11 BSB

a name which — in its original Phoenician spelling — comes from a question uttered during a prominent religious liturgy for Baal. At the end of winter, when this Canaanite deity's annual return from the underworld after triumphing over Death was eagerly anticipated, his followers would gather outside a cave. They would cry out, 'Where is the prince?', thus summoning him forth from his imprisonment. The Hebrew spelling of Jezebel allows for multiple plays on words: it can mean both *where is the Lord?* and *where is the dung?*

Historically, Jezebel was the queen of Samaria. She dined with four hundred and fifty prophets of Baal and four hundred prophets of Asherah — these priests, amply supported by her bounty through a devastating famine, were killed during the confrontation with Elijah on Mount Carmel. The very heart of Israelite idolatry was summed up in Jezebel's name, *where is the Lord?*, with its expectation that Baal's return ensured renewed fertility for the earth after the austerity of winter.

Jesus entirely subverts this religious ritual, exposing it — through both His death and His resurrection — as a shadowy counterfeit. He'd set Himself up to unmask Baal as a fraud, just as previously He'd tackled Asherah's claim to be 'She who walks on water' and Tammuz's right to be titled 'The Bread Come Down from Heaven'. He'd deliberately chosen His moment when, during His trial before the Sanhedrin, Caiaphas had asked Him: 'Are you the Messiah?

'I am,' said Jesus. 'And you will see the Son of Man sitting at the right hand of the Mighty One and coming on the clouds of heaven.'[2]

2.
Mark 14:61–62 NIV

It was this claim to be 'the Cloud-Rider' that led directly led to His death. Caiaphas, seemingly jubilant at Jesus' admission, immediately proclaimed that those in the judgment hall had no further need of witnesses. Jesus had condemned Himself out of His own mouth. Jesus has quoted the vision of the prophet Daniel:

'Behold, with the clouds of heaven there came one like a son of man, and He came to the Ancient of Days and was presented before Him. And to Him was given dominion and glory and a kingdom, that all peoples, nations, and languages should serve Him; His dominion is an everlasting dominion, which shall not pass away, and His kingdom one that shall not be destroyed.'[3]

3.
Daniel 7:13–14 ESV

As Michael Heiser points out,[4] the prevailing understanding of this passage in first century Judea was linked up with that of the heavenly council in Psalm 89. That meant, as far as the Sanhedrin was concerned, Jesus had basically identified Himself as co-regent with Yahweh.

But there was more than simply a claim to be equal with God. There was an implicit and subtle attack on Baal, the king that Asherah wanted one of her brood of young lions to replace. Baal not only claimed the title 'Rider of the Clouds'[5] but was also a co-regent with the chief Canaanite deity.

4.
Michael Heiser, *The Unseen Realm: Recovering the Supernatural Worldview of the Bible*, Lexham Press 2015; also youtube.com/watch?v=JzAa5nZsbmE

One by one, Jesus pursued the godlings of the nations, ripping up their claims to names, titles, positions and histories. Step by step,

5.
http://emp.byui.edu/satterfieldb/ugarit/The%20Epic%20of%20Baal.html

He showed Himself the only begotten, only legitimate Son of the Most High. Despite the evidence, when He was raised from the dead and showed Himself the true heir of the Father, the high priest and the princes of the land were nowhere to be seen. Such high-born, aristocratic witnesses were replaced by a reformed prostitute, as perhaps prophesied by the exquisitely ironic words of Jeremiah:

The priests did not ask, 'Where is the Lord?' Those who taught My word ignored Me, the rulers turned against Me, and the prophets spoke in the name of Baal, wasting their time on worthless idols.[6]

Mary Magdalene is Jezebel redeemed.[7] The very name Jesus gave her testifies to that. It's my belief that her name does not refer to the place she comes from, since she is consistently called '*The Magdalene*' — which in English means 'The Watchtower'. Just as with the giving of the related name 'Cephas' to Simon, there are multiple allusions built into the name. More than one Hebrew word means *watchtower*. Another is 'Samaria' — the capital of the Kingdom of Israel and the place where King Ahab built a temple of Baal for his wife, Jezebel.

Mary Magdalene's name as well as her words evoke the legacy of Samaria and its people. She was a Jew but, at the resurrection, she

6.
Jeremiah 2:8 NLT

was nonetheless a special representative of the Samaritans and the Canaanites, as well as the general representative of mankind. She wasn't chosen because she came from the most noble of those races; she was chosen despite her disreputable background.

Because Mary was the first to tell the apostles of the empty tomb and the words of the angels that Jesus had risen, she is often called the 'Apostle to the Apostles'. Often overlooked as a consequence is her role as kingmaker.

A week before her meeting in the garden with Jesus, she had anointed His head with oil of myrrh, watered His feet with her tears and dried them with her hair. The following day Jesus rode into Jerusalem on a donkey to the wild acclamation of the crowds who wanted to make Him king. Just as Solomon, son of David, rode a donkey on the day

7.
See *Dealing with Ziz: Spirit of Forgetting* for an in-depth explanation of this statement as well as my following comment that Jesus gave her the name 'Magdalene'.

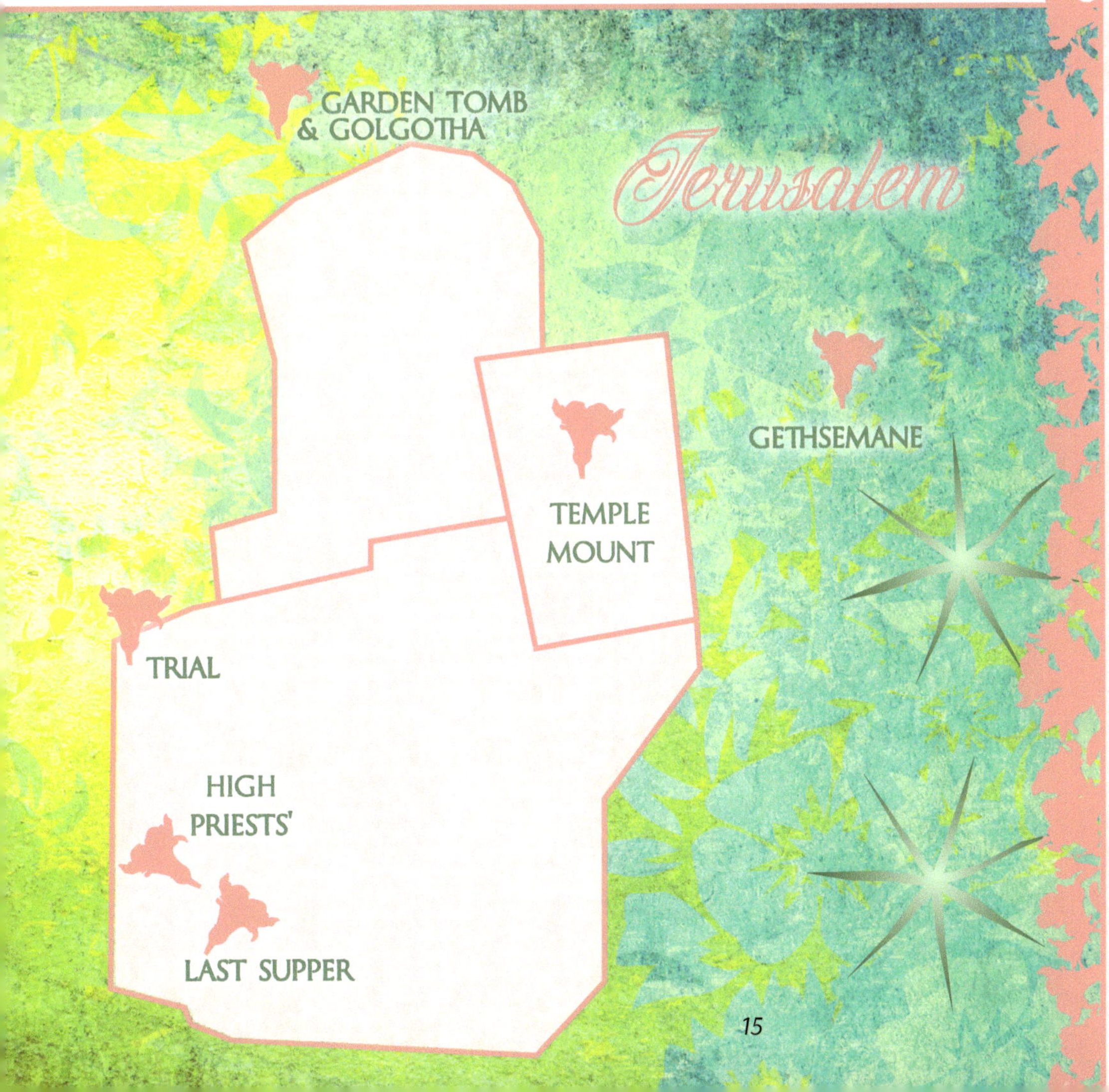

8.
1 Kings 1:33

He was recognised as a king,[8] so too does Jesus, son of David. Mary's role in anointing Jesus mirrored that of Zadok the priest and Nathan the prophet in the past.

As well as the kingmaker, Mary represents the Bride of Christ. She covenanted with Jesus through the oil she smeared on Him. Oil covenants were rare but far from unknown. She broke open her alabaster jar of spikenard and myrrh, and was consequently subjected to a torrent of criticism for her extravagance and thoughtless waste. Yet her reckless, lavish action is as nothing to that of Nicodemus. If she was profligate, then he was a hundred times more so. Because that's the amount of myrrh he brought to the burial of Jesus.

Myrrh was the 'oil of joy' normally used at the consummation of a marriage. Now Nicodemus had been present at the crucifixion, along with John and the three Marys: Mary, the mother of Jesus; Mary, the wife of Cleopas; and Mary Magdalene. He was there when Jesus said, *'It is finished!'*

In Aramaic, this is a single word with overtones of *consummation*: 'kalah.' And it's one of those many words with another meaning.

In this case, it also means *my bride.* Brian Simmons, in the Passion Translation, brings out this dual meaning by translating John 19:30 as: *'It is finished, My bride!'*

It resonates with the power of *'It is done!'* as Jesus sits on His throne, saying: *'Behold I make all things new!'*

> *'It is done! I am the Alpha and the Omega, the beginning and the end.'* [9]

In Greek, *done* is 'gegonan', *to come into being, to be born.*

9. Revelatiuon 21:6

It's not just about a wedding, it's about being born. Mary Magdalene probably heard the gasp from Nicodemus when the side of Jesus was pierced by a Roman lance and separated blood and water flowed out. In a sudden, mind-shattering revelation, he would have realised he'd just witnessed what Jesus meant when He'd talked about having to be 'born again' of water and the Spirit.

In Greek, the word for *blood* is also the word for *spirit.* So as blood/spirit and water flowed from the pierced side of Jesus, he must have been overcome by the knowledge he'd been present at a birth. A natural birth comes about with the breaking of water and with blood, while the spiritual birth Jesus spoke of comes from water and the Spirit. But this is not simply any birth: Nicodemus would have known it's not normal for people to be born through the pierced side of a man. In fact, as an esteemed teacher in Israel, he would have been conscious that it had only ever happened once before in all of history. Nicodemus would have realised he had witnessed an event as momentous as the creation of Eve.

The Bride of the Second Adam has to be born by faith from under His heart, just as the Bride of the First Adam was taken from the rib under his heart.

This is why it's both wedding and birth. Nicodemus wasted no time as soon as he grasped the implications. He needed to prepare for a wedding, not a funeral. And for the consummation of a wedding, it was culturally necessary to have the oil of joy: myrrh. In a staggering

display of faith, he must have sent out servants to scour Jerusalem for a hundred *litra* of it. The chances he had so much myrrh — worth a million dollars in today's money — in his back shed at home are next to nil. By spending the equivalent of one hundred years of wages for an ordinary labourer, he witnessed to the whole of Jerusalem through the oil-dealers: 'The Bridegroom of all creation is coming!' (John 19:39) He was making everything ready to celebrate the wedding of the new Eve.[10]

Nicodemus brought so much myrrh to the tomb that the nearby garden would have been fragrant with wafts of its aroma. But Nicodemus had not been the only contributor to this wedding. The Marys had brought along spices as well. Between them, they had fulfilled prophecy in the last two verses of the Song of Songs. They had quite literally created the 'mountains of spices' for the advent of the Bridegroom:

> 'O you who sit in the gardens,
> My companions are listening for your voice–
> Let me hear it!'
>> 'Hurry, my beloved,
>> And be like a gazelle or a young stag[11]
>> On the mountains of spices.'[12]

An angel of the Lord descended from heaven...
The guards trembled in fear of him.

Matthew 28:2-4 BSB

10.
This section borrows its concepts very heavily from the article on 'Nicodemus' by Arie Uittenbogaard at abarim-publications.com.

11.
The word translated *gazelle* is the same word as *glory*, and that translated *stag* can also be *oak, ram, pillar, mighty man* or even, at not too great a stretch *morning star*. Its meaning is simply *strong leader*, so its translation depends on context. In terms of the resurrection, Jesus was a *strong leader*: as our Captain, He was the firstborn from the dead.

12.
Song of Songs 8:13-14 NAS

13.
Song of Songs 6:1 ESV

14.
This is how and where that *'He disarmed the rulers and authorities and disgraced them publicly; He triumphed over them...'* Colossians 2:15 HCSB

When Jesus mends history, He doesn't do it by halves. Eden is not only reversed but the Marriage of the Lamb is rehearsed. Mary's words, *'They have taken my Lord away, and I don't know where they have put Him,'* echo the wedding scene in the Song of Songs when the friends of the Bride ask: *'Where has your beloved gone, O most beautiful among women? Where has your beloved turned, that we may seek Him with you?'* [13]

Other ancient echoes resound in this tiny sliver of conversation between Jesus and Mary. Recall that Canaanite religion has been despoiled by evoking the ritual of Baal's return from his annual imprisonment in the underworld. The name 'Baal' means *lord, master, husband*.

Jesus appropriated not just the sacred history of Baal but his mythic titles as well. In effect He said that nothing whatsoever belonged to Baal — not his legend, not his liturgy, not his titles, not even his name.[14] Jesus had defeated Baal in a war of 'herem': one devoted to total destruction.[15]

Not content with this mythic appropriation, there's still more. Almost all of the legend of the goddess Angelos is lost to us — but the fragments we have mean that its significance wouldn't have been lost on the Roman soldiers present. It's unlikely they would have known about the local godling Baal, but they probably did know the Greek story of Angelos, whose name means *angel* and who was sent to the underworld for stealing myrrh from the queen of Olympus. The critical elements — angel, myrrh and underworld — appear in the Resurrection story and perhaps figure as part of the reason the soldiers fell down, stunned with fear.[16]

Through His death and resurrection, Jesus accomplished the salvation of the world. John the apostle said at the end of his gospel that, if all that Jesus did were written down, the whole world would not be big enough to contain the volumes needed to tell the story. The same is true, I believe, of what Jesus achieved through His work of salvation. This essay focuses on just one aspect: the healing of history. But there is so much more. I am conscious of barely scratching the surface, even of this topic.

15.
The Hebrew word 'herem' or 'charam' means to *devote to total destruction*. This sense of utter annihilation is one of the meanings given for Hermon, the mountain above Caesarea Philippi. The shrine of Pan here is sometimes equated with that of Baal Aliyan, the godling whose death was suggested as a reason for the sons of Asherah, the 'young lions', to rejoice—since one of them would have a chance of taking his throne.

16.
The victory of Jesus, in despoiling the principalities of the nations, also included as a war trophy the Canaanite thunder deity known as Resheph. Responsible for both plague and healing and given the title *'door-warden of the sun'*, he was also called *'lord of the garden'* by the Phoenicians. So there is no surprise Jesus would retrieve and redeem this title in a garden at dawn.

Resheph had antlers and was symbolised by a stag or a gazelle. The particular combination – *door-warden of the sun* together with *stag* – suggests the name of the *morning star* in Hebrew. Beautiful and unusual, that name is 'ayelet hashachar', meaning *deer at the dawn of the day*. This is heading of the Psalm 22, a prophecy of the crucifixion and the vindication of Jesus. It also links back to the last verse of the *Song of Songs* where the stag on the mountain of spices is mentioned.

This healing is remarkable for its simplicity. It simply requires the essence of the right question: 'Where is the Lord?'

When Jesus healed history, His actions ranged across a spectrum from the outrageously spectacular to the superlatively simple. On the one hand, He cast a legion of demons out of a man to heal the land of the Gadarenes; on the other, He asked for a drink of water to heal the history of Shechem. Here too in the garden there is an extraordinary and complex healing that hinges on a simple request: to know where the Lord is.

The question picks up the thread of a series of traumatic ruptures in human history: beginning with the circumstances of mankind's fall in Eden, moving on to the worship of other gods introduced — at a state level if not a private one — by the queen of Samaria and reinforced later by the shrine to Pan at Caesarea Philippi.

Through this encounter in the garden, Jesus shows us that, whatever our stage of faith, the healing of history is not beyond us. It is not such a high calling we can sit back and think it is so impossibly lofty a gift we will never have the grace or the talent to make a difference.

We may not have the level of faith to perform the miraculous kind of signs — like casting out demons into pigs — that indicate a region has been claimed back for God as well as cleared of the *genius loci* inhabiting it.[17] Or perhaps we may have. But, whether we do or not, we are not excused from the task. Because even the weakest of us surely has the mustard-seed of faith required to ask a question as simple as: 'Where is my lord?'

17.
'Genius loci' is Latin for *the spirit of a place.*

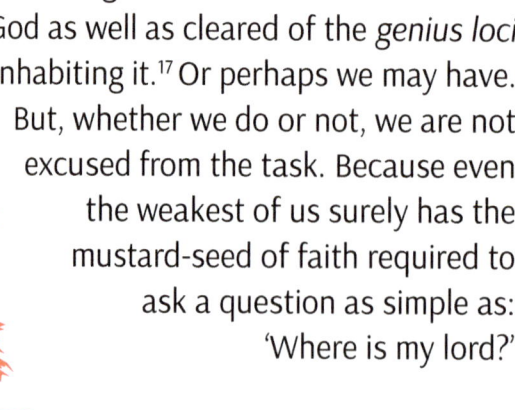

*At dawn on the first day of the week,
Mary Magdalene and the other Mary went to look at the tomb.
There was a violent earthquake, for an angel of the Lord came down from heaven and
… rolled back the stone.*

Matthew 28:1–2 NIV

Discussion Questions:

(1) Consider just a few of the echoes resonating in the conversation of Jesus and Mary in the garden:

- Eden reversed
- The marriage of the Lamb rehearsed
- New birth dispersed
- Canaanite religion despoiled
- Mythic shadows dispelled
- Sacred titles and names appropriated

    (a) Which of these speaks to your heart most strongly?

    (b) Which speaks to your mind most strongly?

(2) To be 'born again', we enter the wound in the pierced side of Jesus. We do this by faith. In so doing, we become the second Eve, drawn from the side of the second Adam. Here we are protected, close to His heart, held to Him in covenantal oneness. Have you accepted the invitation of Jesus to be 'born again' of water and the Spirit?

(3) Where is Jesus asking you to heal history? If you are a redeemed child of God, the healing of history is part of your calling — so if you don't know the answer to this question, ask the Holy Spirit.

RAYER:

Heavenly Father, You are the real healer of history. In a similar way to Jesus responding to Your call to heal the history of His land, I ask that You use me to heal my heritage.

But my own history — the history of my bloodline and generational stream — needs healing first. I am broken and fractured — yet You can use cracked pots for Your purposes. It is the testimony of history that You can and You do offer Jesus' perfect work of healing and salvation through imperfect believers like me. Still I do need to be working out my salvation with fear and trembling and seeing to it that my own generational line is set in order.

Father, so often I do not know where to begin. I have no idea what really happened in my parent's lives — let alone what has happened in the generations before them. And I have even forgotten most of what happened in my own life. It has all been lost in the mists of time. Yet the residue still affects my family daily. Occasionally I hear spoken curses echoing down the years. I am sure they were not meant as a curse but they did become one. Words that cut the heart have had a negative effect on my life and the life of my family. I know they have been in the family line for hundreds of years.

Father, I acknowledge that sin is not wiped out by time. I realise it is only by repentance and the blood of Jesus. But I have been slow to apply His grace to me. I am truly sorry for and repent of having used such words myself. Father, they were so familiar to my family I didn't recognise their power. It was as though they were 'throwaway' statements.

I forgive all in my generations for their use of such words and ask your blessing for my forebears. I ask You to cleanse all in my family with the precious blood of Jesus and to wash down the generational lines with the clean and living water of the Holy Spirit and sluice away all that is not of You.

Father, I today consciously come out of agreement with the satan and I re-commit to the power and authority of Jesus. I ask Jesus to take me into the wound in His side, and to hold me close to His heart. I ask Him to hide me there in the secret place and give me refuge, completely safe from all the power of the enemy. I ask for the unutterable privilege of being born from above by water and the spirit through His pierced side.

And I ask this in the His name, the name of Jesus of Nazareth — Your beloved and chosen Son and my Saviour—and I thank and praise You for the way He modeled the healing of history for us to follow.

Amen

Christ, our Passover,
was sacrificed for us.
Therefore let us keep the feast.

1 Corinthians 5:7-8 NKJV

EMMAUS

So they went on and the sun set as they neared Gibeah in
Benjamin. There they stopped to spend the night.

 Judges 19:14–15 NIV

 Luke 24:29 NAS

"Stay with us, for it is getting toward
evening, and the day is now nearly over."

THE ROAD

A narrative retelling of the background to the journey to Emmaus from the perspective of Mary, the wife of Cleopas and disciple of Jesus.

I have never seen an angel.

Across the years, I wondered why I — alone of all the family — was being denied such a beautiful and terrible vision. Yet more often I wondered if I — alone of all the family — was being spared a beautiful and terrible delusion.

The first I ever heard of anyone seeing an angel was from my husband's brother. As is our custom, he was building a house for his betrothed at the time. And as each Shabbat evening approached, he would oil his carpentry and stonemasonry tools before joining us for the meal. Of course, he would time his arrival to be there just as the sun set, so he could watch me light the lamp and recite the blessing.¹

But this Shabbat he was late. My husband wasn't going to miss such a rare opportunity to tease his twin. He bounced to the door in welcome: 'Late for your birth, little brother. Late for your dinner, little brother. May you be late to greet the grave, little brother.'

I waited for the usual bantering response: 'What would you do without me to pick up after you, greybeard?'

But there was silence. I knew then something was wrong. His eyes were downcast and troubled. The radiant happiness that had characterised him for the last few months was gone. I brought out

---

1. It is normally the woman of a household who will preside at the beginning of a Sabbath—or Shabbat—ceremony.

2. Matthew 1:19

3.
The Bible uses 'sister' and 'brother' to cover a wide range of family relationships, including full blood siblings, half-siblings and in-laws. John 19:25, while a little ambiguous in its wording, seems to indicate that Mary, the wife of Clopas, who is generally regarded as being the same as Cleopas, is the sister of Mary, mother of Jesus. Since it is highly unlikely there would be two women of the same name in a family, this other Mary seems to be her sister-in-law.

4.
Daniel 8:17

the extra wine jug and motioned my husband to take Joseph up to the roof where they could have some privacy. Then I fed the children and shooed them off to bed before taking a plate of broiled fish, matzah and olive oil up to the men.

The first word I heard was 'divorce'.

I was stunned. Dear pious, gentle, God-fearing Joseph planning a *divorce*?[2] And was asking my clueless husband Cleopas as to the best way to go about it? What on earth had happened?

I was soon able to work it out as I listened. Mary was with child. According to the confusing story Joseph was telling, she'd seen an angel. Yeah, *right*. I tried not to roll my eyes at his tangled tale of how she got pregnant after being overshadowed by the Holy Spirit.

It was obvious Joseph didn't have the foggiest notion what to do. Every idea he came up with about getting a 'quiet' divorce was clearly going to make things worse. 'Right,' I said, taking a hand for what was to prove the first of many times, 'listen to me, brother.[3] You can't send her away. There'll be more rumours flying than there are about Herod dallying with Caesar's wife.' I carefully did not mention any rival for Mary's affections. If she'd been raped, why didn't she admit it? Why concoct such an unbelievable story?

I started to point out some practicalities. 'If you want to protect her reputation and keep her safe, who are you going to send with her? She needs a guardian.'

'She's capable. I thought I could give her the money to set herself up in a little business...'

'Where? In Cana? In Capernaum? In Sepphoris? Doesn't matter where it is in Galilee, the entire world will know you've shuffled her away before the opening day is half over.'

Joseph's head drooped. 'So...?'

'More than anything else at the moment you need to buy yourself some time. To find out what's actually happened. You need to get over the shock and start thinking straight. So you need some mental space to consider your options.' I was inexpressibly sorry for him. There were *no* good options. None at all. And, with that thought, I suddenly found myself taking more than a hand in the situation. My whole arm dived in, right up to my elbow. 'Brother, I tell you what I'll do. I'll escort her to her aged cousin. No one will be suspicious of that.'

And that is how I came to travel with Mary to visit her elderly relative, Elizabeth, and how I came to know Jesus even before He was born. I never questioned Mary's story, never expressed my doubts. Just showed my curiosity about what an angel looked like.

Dazzling, she said. *Indescribably dazzling. A voice like many waters.* My suspicions grew at the vagueness of it all. She said she'd been visited by Gabriel. No less than the same holy one as had visited the great prophet Daniel![4]

5.
Traditional home of Elizabeth and Zechariah, a village once outside of Jerusalem, now within the city walls. The name is thought to mean *spring of the vineyard*.

EMMAUS   GIBEAH

JERUSALEM

BETHLEHEM

Yes, my doubts grew. But so did my confusion. Mary was a good match for Joseph. Pious and gentle, just like her betrothed, but also — to my deep bafflement — astonishingly innocent. She seemed to know less than nothing about sexual intimacy. Could she be deluded? Not quite the full shekel? Was she even pregnant?

She sang. Oh, she sang. All the way from Nazareth to Ein Karem.[5] She picked wildflowers as we went — the rose of Sharon was her favourite, and the frothy sprays of blossoms from the manna ash. 'The rose,' she said, 'is the Child. In the old language, the name of the rose is *overshadowed by God's love*.[6] That is who the Child is. The One who came to me through the overshadowing of God's love. The manna is the Child too. For He is the Bread from Heaven.'

I smiled. And said nothing. And thought to myself: *loony*. I came to love her dearly on the journey but I still thought she was touched in the head. And a deep danger to herself. She spoke heresy without even realising it. 'The Bread Come Down From Heaven' is a title belonging to the harvest godling Tammuz.[7]

I tried to hush her but she didn't hear me. She was in her own world most of the time.

Things soon became more complicated. The question over Mary's pregnancy was answered the moment we arrived at Ein Karem.

6.
See abarim-publications.com/Meaning/Sharon.html

7.
Tammuz was a Chaldean deity who was associated with harvests. He was the consort of Asherah, the goddess known as 'She who walks on water.' Jesus directly challenged this pair for their titles on the same day and, through the miracle of the loaves and fishes as well as the miracle of walking on water, reclaimed them and restored them to His Father. See *Like Wildflowers, Suddenly*, the first book in this series, for more insights into this confrontation. During the second century, after the end of the Bar Kokhba rebellion and the razing of Jerusalem by the Emperor Hadrian, both Jewish and Christian pilgrimage sites were deliberately defiled. A shrine for Tammuz as the 'Bread of Heaven' was erected in Bethlehem, *house of bread*, at the very place Jesus was believed to have been born.

The Holy Spirit will come upon you ...

... and the power of the Most High will overshadow you.

Luke 1:36 NASB

8.
Luke 1:42–44

Elizabeth was overjoyed to see her and shouted the news to the whole world. 'But why am I so favoured,' she called out, 'that the mother of my Lord should come to me? As soon as the sound of your greeting reached my ears, the baby in my womb leaped for joy.'⁸

I was speechless. Elizabeth was expecting too? I was thrilled that, at long last, the desire of her heart was about to be fulfilled. And then, as we finally settled down after another spontaneous song from Mary magnifying the Lord, then came the news that sent my mind spinning. Re-assessing. Elizabeth's husband had also seen an angel. When he'd been offering the prayers at the altar of incense.⁹

And the angel was Gabriel. Could it be? Of course not. No. No. No. They were all hallucinating. Surely.

I wanted to have a word with Zechariah, curious as to whether his description of Gabriel matched Mary's description. But he was voiceless. The angel apparently had taken his speech from him for doubting. I spent that night in a state of restless fear. Would an angel rob me of my voice for doubting?

But when I woke, after just an hour's hazy sleep, my voice was perfectly normal. So, satisfied that Mary was in safe hands, I set off back to Nazareth that very morning. I honestly don't remember the trip. It's all a blur in my mind. I was preoccupied with trying

9.
In the time of Jesus, there were so many descendents of Levi that many of them knew they would never be able to serve in the Temple. It has been estimated there were eight thousand priests and ten thousand Levites (see, for example, Darrell L Bock, *Acts*, Baker Academic). In an attempt at fairness, service at the Temple by ordinary priests was determined by lot and was never repeated. So when Zechariah was offering prayers at the altar of incense, it was for him a once-in-a-lifetime event. In a wonderful parallelism, the last person mentioned as seeing an angel in the temple was also a priest named Zechariah. (See Zechariah 6:5.)

to process what I'd learned from Elizabeth and Zechariah. Trying to decide whether I believed it. It took until the end of the second day's walk to come to the sure and definite conclusion that I'd married into a family of crazies. The entire lot of them were beset by messianic fantasies.

But that realisation was terrifying. My thoughts darted to the rebel shepherd Athronges who'd set himself up as king, created his own council and placed a diadem on his head. With his three brothers he'd raised an army against Herod Archelaus as well as our Roman overlords. Just a year ago, they'd had a notable victory at Emmaus. But now it was all over: the brothers were prisoners, the rebellion quashed and Athronges, the messianic claimant, had vanished.[10]

I wanted my family safe. Not in prison. Not beheaded. Not crucified. Not enslaved.

I rushed into Cleopas' arms as soon as I arrived back home in Nazareth. The children were out playing so I told him the news, told him everything — my doubts, my suspicions, my total and absolute terror. He comforted me as he assembled the evening meal and made me sit and watch. I didn't protest. It was Rosh Chodesh, the new moon, and my special holiday. Not every man in our village gave his wife the day off each month but my husband's family, despite their crazy messianic pretensions, were darlings in this regard. They honoured the woman according to the ancient tradition that came down from the time of our people's desert wanderings.[11]

10.
See wikipedia.org/wiki/Athronges

Because Cleopas was busy, I didn't notice his distraction at first. But then I realised he was waiting for the right moment to tell me something. 'What is it?' I demanded. 'What's happened?'

'Joseph has been visited by an angel. In a dream. What Mary says is all true.'

I gasped. And for a second or two I was tempted to believe that angels were flitting around, working overtime on special delivery messages for my in-laws. But then common sense re-asserted itself and I knew it was all illusion. We were, after all, exceptionally ordinary people. Not royalty, not priests, not lawyers, not even wealthy traders. Sure, Cleopas and Joseph could trace their ancestors back to king David, but so could thousands of other peasants in Galilee alone.

In fact, it was only a few months later that we had a clear and present demonstration of just how many thousands of others could legitimately call themselves 'son of David'. Caesar Augustus called a census. Naturally we all went together to Bethlehem: Cleopas and me, together with the children, along with Mary and Joseph. She'd returned after three months with Elizabeth. We'd tried to keep her hidden, but our efforts weren't all that effective. The rumour mill was working overtime.

11.
For more information on this monthly holiday for women at the new moon, see Anne Hamilton and Natalie Tensen, *More Precious than Pearls: The Mother's Blessing and God's Favour Towards Women,* Armour Books.

Originally Joseph was insistent on leaving Mary behind in my custody. But she would have none of it. 'Don't you understand?' she railed at him. 'The Child must be born in Bethlehem. Micah prophesied it: "*But you, Bethlehem Ephrathah, though you are small among the clans of Judah, out of you will come for me one who will be ruler over Israel, whose origins are from of old, from ancient times.*"'[12]

Joseph nodded and gave way without another word. So, we all went. I entrusted the birthing stool, the flint knife, the salt and the cloths for swaddling a newborn to my children so I could concentrate on helping Mary. The road to Bethlehem seemed like it stretched on to forever. It was so hard on her. And we all went so much slower because of her.

12.
Micah 5:2 NIV

I thought we'd find some lodging with distant relatives but we realised the futility of that idea, long before we got there. A stream of thousands were passing us by. I didn't need to be a prophet to know that there'd be no accommodation at the inn either. Cleopas went ahead anyway, making enquiries. They were fruitless.

By the way Mary's pains were coming, I realised we would soon need water for the birth. And that made me hope we could pitch a tent by the ancient well. But we were still far off when it became obvious several thousand others had had the same idea. We didn't have a hope of getting anywhere close. At the other end of town, guarding the aqueducts that sluiced water down to Jerusalem, the Roman garrison was a forbidding fortress.[13] Our hearts shrank at the sight.

Mary was nearing her time. Her waters had already broken. Joseph was frantic. Cleopas, bless his dear heart, had a brilliant idea. The lambing tower. He knew about a watchtower overlooking the fields and used by the priests at Passover.[14] It was their holding place so that lambs brought in from the flocks could be examined before the spotless ones were sent to Jerusalem for the temple sacrifice. At this time of year, it might well be empty.

13.
romanaqueducts.info/aquasite/jerusalemAq1/index.html

We got there just in time. I gave the children a jug each and sent them for water from the well; I got Joseph and Cleopas out of the way by telling them to find somewhere we could lay the babe; I got Mary onto the birthing stool and then — well, for me — it was a total

anticlimax. Jesus was born. I cut His umbilical cord with the flint knife. He looked so small, so vulnerable, so... well, *ordinary*. I had somehow hoped for more. For something to crush my doubts.

The men had found a cave behind the watchtower with stone mangers. So once the children had come back with the water, I washed and salted and swaddled the boy. Then we all praised God for the safe delivery and placed him in one of them. I was helping Mary clean and change her garments when the sound of strange voices alerted us to the arrival of company.

14.
Migdal Eder, *tower of the flock*, mentioned in both Micah 4:8 and Genesis 35:21. It was a tradition that this would be the very place where the coming of the Messiah would first be announced. See int.icej.org/news/commentary/tower-flock for more detail.

Mary retreated into the shadows as a group of shepherds crept through the door.[15] They were wary and wide-eyed. 'Is the Messiah here?' one whispered.

'Are you mad? What makes you say that?' I snapped. 'Do you think we're hiding your rebel king Athronges?'

'It's a little baby,' he squeaked. 'That's what the angel said.'

'*Angel?*' I raised my fists. How come everyone sees angels except me? Has the whole world gone stark raving mad? '*Angel!*' I held back a swear word Cleopas would have been astonished I even knew. 'You

15.
If the birth did indeed occur at Migdal Eder, then these shepherds would most likely have been in the employ of the Temple at Jerusalem. They would have been highly aware of all the messianic symbolism surrounding this tower. In late Hebrew, the word 'tela', meaning *lamb*, also means *young boy*.

think I'd believe a *shepherd*?' My face, I'm now ashamed to say, was a twisted sneer. My tone dripped scorn. No one trusted shepherds. The lowest of the low, even their sworn testimony was inadmissible in court.

'Let's go,' the shepherd said to his companions, backing off at my aggressive attitude. 'We've made a mistake.'

Two of the shepherds were women. One of them confronted me boldly as she yanked the man around. 'There's no mistake.' She glared at me. 'We. Saw. Angels. This after all is Bethlehem, where shepherds can become kings, and all things are possible.'

I gaped, realising she wasn't being sarcastic. The other woman took the opportunity to stalk right up to me. 'And their leader said we would know the saviour by the sign of swaddling clothes and being in a manger.'

'That's why we thought of this lambing tower,' the other woman said. 'We know there are mangers here.'

They waited. I produced my fiercest scowl.

'We owe no allegiance to Athronges,' the man said earnestly. 'Nor to Herod. Nor to Caesar Augustus. Only to the Name, blessed be he. Lady, listen. We mean no harm. The Lord's angel hosts, they seem very joyful. They're celebrating tonight.'

His eyes held such yearning appeal that I could not be angry with him for seeing angels — yes, angel*s* plural; not just one but multitudes. Undone by the soul-deep brokenness and loneliness I could see behind the radiant hope on the women's faces, I took them all down into the cave and showed them the babe. The impossibly ordinary infant who was so tiny and no-different-to-a-million-other-newborns. They were thrilled at the sight and told the story of the angels over and over. After a while it began to grate on my nerves.

The census done, Cleopas and I headed back to Nazareth. Joseph decided to stay on in Bethlehem. His plan was to wait until the gossip in Nazareth moved on to topics other than Mary and the questionable legitimacy of Jesus. We heard from him occasionally

over the next few years; once a strange message about magi from the east who'd brought gifts of gold, frankincense and myrrh; and then, a short while later, an even stranger message about going to live in Egypt because an angel told him so in a dream.[16]

The obsession with angels irritated me. Cleopas set about finishing the house Joseph had almost completed. He was always convinced Joseph would return. It angered me that he'd work on his brother's house when so much needed to be done around our own. I almost lost it with him several times: what makes you so sure he'll be back? Did some smartypants angel tell you?

But then the day came when — miraculously — they returned. And seeing the sturdy young boy, Jesus, whom I'd last held as a sweet newborn, my heart melted. And seeing the joy on Mary's face when she spotted me, I found an answering joy flowering on my own. And then seeing Joseph, and the shaded wariness in his eyes, I was so glad Cleopas had finished the house. I ran to them and folded them all, somehow, into a welcoming hug. They were family, after all.

I hoped the crazy looniness had been a phase that could be relegated to the past. And for many quiet and beautiful years — through the additions of more children and the passing of our dear Joseph — it seemed so. No sign of a messianic complex. As I regarded my nephew

16. Matthew 2:13

Jesus over that time, I would have said He was contented and compliant. Others would have called him *obedient*, but I sometimes wondered if He was *too* obedient. Too dutiful. Too conforming. And too pious by half. He'd go out constantly into the hills to pray.

He had a knowing way about him. He would gaze at me, silent and solemn-eyed, as if He knew something about me that I didn't. Then He'd say: 'Aunt Myrrh, you will remember, won't you?'

And, transfixed by that look, I'd assure Him I would. Even though I wasn't sure what I was supposed to remember. Aunt Myrrh was his pet name for me. Because his mother and I had the same name — Mary — He'd always called me Myrrh to distinguish between us.

It took me a while but eventually I realised the question always came at the same time of year. We were at the synagogue one time, and the reading was from the Song of Solomon which, blessed be the Name, was symbolic enough for the erotic elements to go right over the children's heads.

Again the gaze, silent and solemn-eyed, and the question: 'Aunt Myrrh, you will remember, won't you?'

'What am I supposed to remember, Jesus?' I asked Him.

17.
Song of Solomon 8:14 NIV

Before the dawn breezes blow
and the night shadows flee,
I will hurry to the
mountain of myrrh.

Song of Solomon 4:6 NLT

'Your prophecy. You must be ready.'

'*My* prophecy? Just for *me*?' I was laughing inside.

'Yes, just for you, Aunt Myrrh,' He said. 'But be careful. Another will take your place in building the mountain of spices if you're not prepared.' If possible, His gaze became even more earnest. But there was a twinkle in His eye.

His words caused me to ponder the very last line of the Song of the Son of David in my heart. '*Come away, my beloved, and be like a gazelle or a young stag on the mountains of spices.*'17 What did *that* mean? What were the mountains of spices? How was I to build them?

Despite the strangeness, perhaps even because of the strangeness, I thought all was well. If making mysterious applications of Scriptural prophecy was going to be the limit of Jesus' unusual behaviour, there was nothing to worry about. He was basically a normal boy.

As the years went by, I began to believe that both Mary and Joseph had kept — yes, had very wisely kept — all the stories of angels and shepherds and magi and Holy-Spirit-overshadowing from him.

18.
Luke 4:18–21 NIV

But then came the incident at the synagogue. True, I'd heard gossip coming out of Cana about a miracle at a wedding. Something about water changing to wine. But it was such a garbled tale, I'd dismissed it as the product of a drunken delirium. But the synagogue was different. I was there when, as a new rabbi, he unrolled the scroll of the prophet Isaiah and raised his voice: '*The Spirit of the Lord is on me, because he has anointed me to proclaim good news to the poor. He has sent me to proclaim freedom for the prisoners and recovery of sight for the blind, to set the oppressed free, to proclaim the year of the Lord's favour.*' He rolled up the scroll and sat down. '*Today this scripture is fulfilled in your hearing.*'18

19.
Luke 4:29

The accusation of blasphemy almost got him killed. The crowd dragged him out to the cliff, ready to throw him over.19 But as the judges were called, Cleopas, together with Jesus' brothers, managed to slide him back into their midst so he could get away.

We had a decision to make. Cleopas sat us down during Shabbat

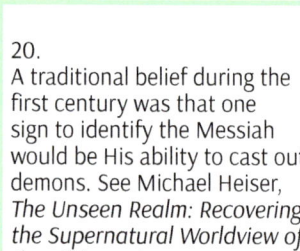

20.
A traditional belief during the first century was that one sign to identify the Messiah would be His ability to cast out demons. See Michael Heiser, *The Unseen Realm: Recovering the Supernatural Worldview of the Bible*, Lexham Press.

21.
Another traditional belief of the time concerned a royal messiah known as the 'Son of David' and also a war messiah known as the 'Son of Joseph'. John's gospel uses that second title, indicating Jesus fulfils both roles, though in unexpected ways—since it was anticipated that the 'Son of Joseph', the war messiah, would come from the tribe of either Ephraim or Manasseh (the sons of the patriarch Joseph).

to talk it over. Since Joseph's death, he'd been responsible for Mary until Jesus came of age. In theory, he'd long ago handed over that mantle but, while Jesus had been studying to become a rabbi, in practice things had remained unchanged.

The question was: do we support not just Mary but Jesus himself? There were obvious dangers but, as Cleopas pointed out, clearly Jesus was the Messiah.

'What makes you so sure?' I asked, keeping my voice neutral.

'No prophet has ever cast out demons,' Cleopas pointed out. 'Yet it has always been prophesied that, when the Messiah comes, that will be His sign.'[20]

Yes, true. But no. *No!* I wanted to shout it out in wild frenzied fury. He is *not* the Messiah. He's nothing like Athronges or Theudas or Hezekiah the bandit chief or his son Judah. Nothing. Think of the ambitions of Simon of Peraea or Judas the Galilean and you'll know Jesus is nothing like that. He can't be the Messiah. Neither the royal messiah, nor the war messiah.[21] He simply can't be.

But, of course, we supported Him. He was family. There were others too who helped as the years went by — and they startled me by the

risks they took. The Magdalene — she was understandable since he'd cast seven demons out of her. But I never quite got the reasoning of Joanna, the wife of Herod's steward, or that of the wealthy teacher Nicodemus, who secretly sponsored Jesus and His disciples.

I mention these three in particular because, when everything came crashing down, they still stood by us. I was there, shoulder to shoulder, with Nicodemus and Mary Magdalene in the eerie darkness at the foot of the Cross. It seemed to me that the sun had turned its face from us, too ashamed to witness the crucifixion of heaven's treasure. Jesus, my darling nephew, so innocent and compassionate, was being executed in a travesty of justice.

So I was there to support Mary, His mother, as her heart cracked. I was surprised that my own heart was relatively intact. But perhaps because I'd always held back from belief, I wasn't as devastated as those who'd laid all their hopes of national restoration on him. Because despite all the miracles, the signs, the wonders, the healings, the fleeing demons, I still didn't see my nephew as the Messiah. Not because he was my nephew. No, not that. Because he wasn't political. He wanted to love people into life, not rule them with an iron fist.

Looking back, I now know that something in me simply couldn't believe: whether I'd chosen to build a stronghold of disbelief or unbelief or even anti-belief, I don't know. But I do know the moment when it all changed.

It was on the day he died.

Jesus had spoken his last word: 'Kalot!' — '*It is consummated!*'

Nicodemus, next to me, shivered at that final cry. 'Yes, it is finished,'[22] he whispered. 'It's all over.' He slumped forwards. I could feel a dream die within him.

So we were all startled by the riveting announcement of the watching centurion. '*Truly this was the Son of God.*'[23]

A bit late, I thought somewhat cynically.

We waited on his permission to take the body down, but he wasn't giving it until he got authority from Pilate. I couldn't comfort either of the other Marys. There was nothing in me.

I leaned instead to listen to Nicodemus, mumbling in grief and loss. 'Why did he speak the word of the Bridegroom?'

He was puzzling about '*kalot*'? Yes, it was the joyful cry of the bridegroom at the consummation of a marriage and I felt a stab of pain that my nephew, never-betrothed, had been forever deprived of the sweet bliss of physical intimacy. I was irritated with Nicodemus for his intellectualising of our family's tragedy. Surely he realised it was unreasonable to expect a dying man to make sense.

After several minutes, a messenger approached the centurion. Immediately taking a lance, he pierced the side of Jesus with the spearhead. Blood and water flowed out.

'Blood and water,' Nicodemus said. 'Spirit and water. As at a birth.'

We waited.

'But birth doesn't happen through the pierced side of a man.' He paused. 'Unless...' Without warning, Nicodemus grabbed my arm and screamed in my face. '*Myrrh*!'

I thought, for a second, that he was yelling my name.

'We need myrrh!' He wrenched off his signet ring and thrust it into my hands. 'Give this to my servants as a sign of your authority. Tell them to buy a hundred pints of myrrh *now*! Immediately! And bring it here before the sun sets.'

His voice was commanding and, even though I knew he'd cracked, I'd

22.
The last word of Jesus on the Cross—in Greek, 'tetelestai'—is usually translated as 'It is finished!' However, it can also mean, 'It is accomplished!' or 'It is paid in full!' or 'It is consummated!' This final option is equivalent to the Hebrew word, 'kalot', which also means 'It is finished!' or 'It is consummated!' In Jewish culture, it was the joyful cry of the Bridegroom at the consummation of a marriage. And, as part of that consummation, the marriage bed called for the aroma of the oil of joy as a sign of blessing on the union. Myrrh was the 'oil of joy'.

spent half my life around people who were varying degrees of crazy. So I just did as he asked.

'Hurry, myrrh, hurry,' he called, as I walked off. I wasn't sure whether he was addressing me by name or summoning the oil itself. A hundred pints—what was he thinking? The extravagance, the profligate waste. I thought of the criticism of the Magdalene just a few days ago for breaking open merely a single pint. Surely Nicodemus had noticed: this was a death, not a wedding. Besides, a hundred pints of the oil of joy — why, that was a *mountain* of the stuff!

I froze, mid-step. The prophecy. The one Jesus had always said was about *me*. About me and the mountain of spices.

I felt, almost as a physical sensation, the chains in my mind break. And I ran. Faster than I'd ever run before. Belief was pouring into my soul like a flood.

Breathless, I got to the house of Nicodemus, delivered his orders and sped back. My feet were wings. We needed more than myrrh. We needed frankincense and nard, aloes and calamus, roses and lilies, cedar and manna ash.

We buried Jesus, with great honour. But we couldn't get the spices in time, even with the aid of Nicodemus and Joseph of Arimathea. I'd left it too late. The one thing Jesus had charged me with — remembering

23.
Matthew 27:54 ESV

to prepare the mountain of spices — was the very thing I'd forgotten.

My heart would sing inside me, rising higher and higher like a lark, and then it would plunge into keening grief. Would he rise on the third day as he'd promised? My belief hadn't stabilised. It was wild and erratic. It danced and it stumbled. It soared and it sank.

We got together — we three Marys — to remember, remember, remember as we mixed the spices on the evening immediately after the Sabbath. Everything was ready for the following morning. We met before dawn, our oil lamps flickering in front of our feet while we carried the baskets of spices on our back. We were outside the walls when the earthquake hit. We later found out it occurred as an angel was rolling back the stone in front of Jesus' tomb. Yes, an angel. The Magdalene ran ahead and saw his dazzling form and heard his wondrous message.

But me? No, of course not.

I'd lost my lamp in the earthquake and was delayed trying to find it again. I realised I shouldn't have tried. The smell of a hundred pints of myrrh wafting across the garden would have been enough to guide me in the right direction.

I had arrived just seconds late. The angel was gone. And the Magdalene was glowing. It wasn't just the light of dawn made her

> As the deer pants for streams of water, so my soul longs after You.
> Psalm 42:1 BSB

24.
Matthew 28:7 NIV

seem that way. She repeated the message she'd been charged to give the disciples: '*He has risen from the dead and is going ahead of you into Galilee. There you will see him.*'[24] She made the rest of us memorise it.

We all hurried back to the Upper Room; and after assuring Peter and John there wasn't a Roman soldier in sight, she ran with them back to look at the scene. The day then began to ebb and flow with news. Peter and John had seen an empty tomb. John had seen a neat, folded linen gravecloth on one side. The Magdalene had seen Jesus in the garden. No one really believed her. But I did.

I said to Cleopas as the afternoon wore on, 'Jesus said he's going to Galilee. But nobody's moving. We have to set an example.'

Cleopas frowned at me. 'You think he's alive?'

'Don't you?'

The frown turned to a stare. 'You've never believed in him.' Then he smiled. 'Oh, you've hid it well all these years. But I've always known. So if you believe at last, dear doubting wife, then I must.'

We were on the road west within the hour. We thought we'd be able to reach Emmaus by nightfall. Emmaus, the town of great and historic victories. Athronges the shepherd had triumphed over the Romans here nearly four decades ago now. And, a century before his insurrection, the mighty Maccabees had routed the Greeks, paving the way for the restoration of the temple, the cleansing of its abominable defilement and the miracle of the multiplying oil.[25]

But as we walked, the doubts set in. As I said, my belief hadn't stabilised. And the fact the disciples clearly didn't believe in Jesus' resurrection unsettled me. I sensed John did, by his remarks about the gravecloth, but Peter still had reservations.

We couldn't help but talk about the day's events as we walked. We tried to keep our voices down. But then, a stranger came up and began to keep pace with us.

Yes, it was Jesus. My nephew. People often wonder how we didn't recognise him — was His resurrected body so different that it was impossible to identify him? Anyone who asks is obviously not familiar with the road from Jerusalem to Emmaus on a late afternoon in spring. The sun is low in the sky, slanting directly into your eyes. You squint but all you can see is a dazzling light-limned shape — and it's hard to pick features out of the contrasting shadow.

As for his voice, in retrospect, I wonder if we didn't recognise it because he was too busy trying to stop laughing. He must have been pushing down that bubble of elation and joy inside as he wondered when we were going to figure out who he was.

As for not greeting us by name, well, I think that was part of the fun for him. His parables had always sparkled with humour—so often lost in translation — but his actions that afternoon bordered on a boyish prank. Yet, even so, his true agenda was much more serious.

25.
The cleansing of the temple after the triumph of the Maccabees is still celebrated annually during the Feast of Hanukkah.

My own story, as most people finally guess, is one of brokenness. My ability to believe — to trust others — was shattered long before Jesus was born. The Magdalene's story in the garden was about fixing the Fall of all mankind — but mine is about mending bent and broken minds, bent and broken hearts, bent and broken lives, bent and broken dreams, bent and broken bodies.

It wasn't until much later that I put all the clues together and realised why I'd felt compelled to urge Cleopas to leave Jerusalem so late that day. We were summoned by the Spirit to re-enact the pages of the past, so that history itself could be healed.

To achieve the mending and upending of the most savage and brutal incident in our entire history, a married couple whose ancestral hometown was Bethlehem needed to be walking the road leading away from Jerusalem in the late afternoon. They had to be going about sixty stadia before seeking lodging for the evening. A servant had to be with them. Jesus himself played that role.

There was one other detail needed, but he'd put that in place less than a week previously. He had created a symbol: the breaking of bread to represent the breaking of a body.

I should have seen it long before I did. The story of brokenness from the scroll of Judges[26] had always touched a raw and sensitive part of my heart. It starts like this: a Levite and his minor wife — a concubine — together with their servant, set out from their hometown of Bethlehem late one afternoon. They're heading for the hill country in the far distance and, as they converse on the journey, they go past the fortress of Jebus — later to become Jerusalem. Eventually they reach a village, Gibeah of Benjamin, just as the sun sets. There they face the prospect of having to spend the night in the open square but finally secure hospitality for the night with an elderly man from another tribe. They are just beginning their meal when some local men surround the house and demand that the Levite be sent out so they can have sex with him.

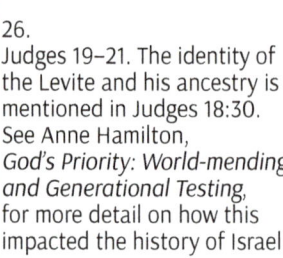

26.
Judges 19–21. The identity of the Levite and his ancestry is mentioned in Judges 18:30. See Anne Hamilton, *God's Priority: World-mending and Generational Testing*, for more detail on how this impacted the history of Israel.

Yes, profound echoes of Sodom here — so it should be no surprise what happens next. The host proposes to send out his daughter. But as it transpires, unlike the events at Sodom, the host and his guest don't have a pair of angels arrive to defend them. Instead things turn obscene and violent when they throw the wife out to appease the attackers. She is gang-raped all night.

At first light, as she is dying, she reaches out to touch the untouchable: the sacred cornerstone where the blood of sacrifice would normally drip down from the lintels and doorposts. Her action accuses all the men involved in this shameful episode: it says, louder than words could ever do, '*I* am your threshold sacrifice.'

Instead of defending her to the death, her husband and the host sacrificed her to save themselves. Under the threshold covenant that was invoked the moment she and her husband stepped over the threshold and accepted the old man's offer of hospitality, the men should have protected her with their lives. But they used her as a commodity to save their own skins.

But that wasn't the worst of it. Her husband then did something even more unspeakable. He cut her body up, like that of an animal, and sent it around the tribes to Israel to call them to war. The inhuman depravity of all the men involved — from the men of Gibeah to the Levite — had always been almost incomprehensibly disturbing to me.

Yet the thing I found most shocking of all was the identity of the Levite. He was Jonathan, grandson of Moses — and with this one stroke, he set in train a series of events that destroyed everything his grandfather took forty years to accomplish. The call to war was never meant to pit one tribe against another — it was there in the event of attack by *external* enemies. The clan brotherhood which Moses and Aaron sacrificed so much to forge never recovered from this diabolical blow.[27]

When the tribe of Benjamin came to defend Gibeah, they were almost totally exterminated: only six hundred men survived, no women or children. The other eleven tribes were belatedly horrified at what they'd done, but that didn't stop them adding to the catastrophe. They went to wipe out an entire town[28] on the other side of the

27.
Jonathan, the grandson of Moses—the Levite who started all this—wisely left the neighbourhood and headed off to the far north where his descendants set up an idolatrous sanctuary with a golden calf. That shrine was at Dan—near Caesarea Philippi. How Jesus healed the history of Dan and Caesarea Philippi is told in the second book in this series, *Bent World, Bright Wings*.

28.
Jabesh Gilead, which may possibly also be known as Tishbe, the hometown of Elijah.

Jordan and killed everyone there except the young unmarried girls. They then presented these girls as trophies of war to the six hundred surviving men so they could rebuild their tribe.

I used to feel soul-stricken thinking of the children and grandchildren of Gibeah in the days when the tribe of Benjamin was rebuilding. Those little ones would have been fathered by bitter, twisted men who had only just survived a near-genocide. Those little ones have been mothered by grieving, resentful women who were trophies of war. Both parents would have been subjected to unfathomable trauma.

And one of those children of Gibeah was Saul, our first king. A great man, no mistake — because, despite his background, he healed many rifts that came from this terrible war. However, he could not overcome the flaws and failures in his nature stemming from the bentness and brokenness of his home town — and even, in many ways, stemming from the nation built on the bent and broken tribal brotherhood.

The legacy of Jonathan's actions at Gibeah cast a vast dark shadow over our history. Half a millennium later, the prophet Hosea lamented that its influence was still strong: *'They have sunk deep into corruption, as in the days of Gibeah.'*[29] This wasn't a throwaway comparison: it was the most intense indictment of evil possible.

29.
Hosea 9:9

So how did Jesus heal this profound stain on the past? There had been centuries of ineradicable iniquity built up higher and higher upon that first violation. How did he stitch history up and bring it into *shalom*?

Was it through the burning of our hearts as we listened to prophecy after prophecy being lined up with the life and sufferings of Jesus? No. Not at all.

The reason I didn't initially notice that Jesus was actually in the process of healing history even as we were walking along was that my expectations, as always, were too great. I was looking for something momentous, and everything about what was happening was too simple.

The women came to the tomb, bringing the spices they had prepared.
Luke 24:1 BSB

I missed it for just that reason: it was exquisitely and elegantly ordinary. All Jesus was doing was walking the same road as the Levite and his wife. Yes, he selected the same time of day. Yes, he fell in with companions who could legally stand in as representatives for those of the past. But he didn't force the matter: he made as if to go on and, if Cleopas and I had chosen not to invite Him to dine with us and urged him to cross the threshold into the house where we were staying, the healing of history would have been aborted.

The mending couldn't be manipulated. It had to be voluntary. We had to offer true and unsolicited hospitality to the shepherd king. Not to a king who, like the shepherd Athronges, left his followers to their fate. And not to a king, who like Judah Maccabeus, was a hammer to his foes. No, to a king who was the Good Shepherd. And to a king who had laid down his life, even for his enemies.

"Did not our hearts burn within us while He talked to us on the road?"
Luke 24:32 ESV

When He finally revealed Himself in the taking and blessing and breaking of bread, all the echoes of the past came crashing into that searing moment. We remembered how Jesus on the night he was betrayed, said, 'This is my body,' as he blessed and broke bread.

The flames in our hearts burned still brighter as we not only recognised him but thought of all the prophecies He'd mentioned during our walk. Our heads buzzing with Scripture, I was finally reminded of another broken body: that of the woman of Bethlehem whose husband used her as a call to war.

As the world tilted and spun, and — awestruck — we took a place in its mending, we turned to Jesus. But he was no longer there.

His voice, though, was echoing in my mind. 'Aunt Myrrh, you will remember, won't you?'

It was as if the words were whirled up and away, then slotted down into the very centre of a huge mosaic. I thought of the other Marys and who they were and their place in the mending. Mary of Bethany, the Magdalene, who'd heard his commendation just a week ago: *'Truly I tell you, wherever the gospel is preached throughout the world, what she has done will also be told, in memory of her.'*[30]

In memory of her.

30.
Matthew 26:13 NIV

Memory. Mary had become the first of the myrrh-bearers when she'd broken open the alabaster jar of myrrh-scented nard to anoint him for his entry into Jerusalem as the son of David. But in doing so, she'd become a memorial, a keeper of memory. We would testify to her memory so her testimony to the resurrection was validated.

But it went back to the dawn of time, just as Nicodemus had recognised. He'd seen the significance of the blood and water coming from the side of Jesus. It *was* a birth. But he also recognised that birth did not normally occur from a man's side. Only once before in all of history had it ever happened: when Eve was drawn from Adam.

All those who'd stood at the foot of the Cross represented the new Adam's bride. That's why Nicodemus had yelled for myrrh. Because he realised the wedding of God to the company of believers had just been consummated.

But now *I* realised there was much, much more to the mountain of myrrh.

You will remember, won't you? I thought Jesus wanted me to remember to prepare the mountains of spices for his death and his wedding. But it was so very much more: he wanted me to remember our conversation on the road to Emmaus. He'd explained so many prophecies to me and Cleopas. He'd made us guardians of that knowledge, custodians of an official interpretation, keepers of His understanding of Himself.

31.
Genesis 2:15

The company of believers had been appointed as the new *shomerim*. God had chosen Adam as his vice-regent and the first *shomer* — the keeper, the guardian, the protector — of earth.[31] The first Adam had failed, but the second Adam would not. We, his Bride, were to be his partners in mending the world. And the reason there were so many myrrh-bearers named Mary was to highlight the restoration of the vice-regency: for our names spoke of keeping, guarding, protecting memory.

As it dawned on me that we'd just been called as the first of the new *shomerim* — to be a role model for generations to come — that burning in my heart flamed higher.

Cleopas and I rushed back to Jerusalem that very evening. We couldn't wait to explain to the others all that we'd suddenly come to realise. Everyone who'd been expecting the Messiah to call us to war was wrong. His call was to *shalom*: to recompense and soundness, welfare and wholeness, peace and prosperity.

That was why I could never believe in the Messiah before. Because his coming wasn't ever going to be about politics or war. Yes, it was going to be an upheaval — but the upheaval of *shalom*, the very thing my heart had always yearned for.

You know, I still have never seen an angel.

But it no longer matters. For I have seen the Messiah.

Notes

Most believers simply accept that Jesus went to Emmaus on the day of His resurrection without ever asking why He would give top priority to a stroll into the country. At face value, as the story is recounted by Luke, He headed out beyond the suburbs, meeting up in the process with two random followers never previously mentioned in the gospel account. He broke some bread and then vanished.

But when we examine the timing — and realise it happens straight after his return from his ascent to the Father — we have to ask: what could possibly be next on the list after undoing the curse of Adam's sin in the garden? He's prioritised this above everything else. So what on earth could have been so damaging that it tore the world apart almost as much as the treason of Adam?

Now certainly Jesus honoured those who had stood by Him at the cross as soon as possible on the day of his resurrection. First He spoke to Mary Magdalene in the garden, then to the disciples on the road to Emmaus, and later that evening He visited His mother and John.

I accept the early Christian tradition identifying the disciple with Cleopas as his wife, and I have written the narrative above from her perspective. Luke kept the identity of Cleopas' companion anonymous. But the early church tradition was quite clear — the unnamed disciple was not only the wife of Cleopas, she was the aunt of Jesus.

John names her as Mary, wife of Clopas, but there are so many Marys in the gospels that Matthew resorts to calling her 'the other Mary'.

Early church tradition also clearly linked the story in the Book of Judges about the Levite and his concubine to the Emmaus journey. This belief in their connection was so strong that Christian scribes slightly amended the Greek wording of Judges 19 to exactly match Luke's description of the walk to Emmaus. The Codex Alexandrinus shows the Greek text of Judges 19:9 was altered to read just like Luke 24:29. According to Carsten Thiede in *Emmaus Mystery: Discovering Evidence of the Risen Christ*, most modern translators have also seen the parallel and given the verses identical wording. This may be true for German editions of the Bible — to which Thiede was obviously referring — but I cannot find that it also holds for English versions.

Now there are a couple of extra threads in this story of Mary and her husband retracing the tragic journey of Jonathan and his concubine — his minor wife — over a millennium previously. That episode is not only the most gruesome in Scripture, it was — the fall in Eden excepted — undoubtedly the most far-reaching. The death of the concubine led to the almost complete annihilation of the tribe of Benjamin. It also led to generations of complex feuding, violence and hatred between the people of Bethlehem and those of Gibeah. The first location is the hometown of David, Israel's second king, and the second location is the hometown of Saul, Israel's first king.

In addition, the concubine's death also led — by circuitous circumstances — to the installation of an idolatrous sanctuary in northern Israel where a golden calf was worshipped. This shrine in the city of Dan, near Caesarea Philippi, was serviced by the descendants of Jonathan.

Jesus stepped into the history of this vile and iniquitous episode and tipped it over completely. He joined a man and his wife — a man with a suitably symbolic name, actually linking him to that shrine in Dan. Cleopas happens to be the male counterpart to the name Cleopatra — the queen of Egypt who just happened to have been deeded the land around Caesarea Philippi some seventy years beforehand. The previous book in this series, *Bent World, Bright Wings*, examines the healing of the history of Caesarea Philippi and its surrounds. Perhaps that was a necessary precursor to this healing at Emmaus.

Jesus summons every one of us, as believers, to the mending of the world, the repair of history, the healing of the land, the restoration of inheritance, the advance of the Kingdom of Love. It might seem beyond us: far too difficult.

We can look at what Jesus did in the garden to reverse the curse of Eden and think: no, not possible. I can't do anything like that.

But Jesus doesn't allow us that excuse. As the walk to Emmaus shows us, the reversal doesn't have to be an overwhelming, taxing, harrowing event. Nor does it have to be one full of delirious fanfare and extended preparation.

At least on our side.

It can be as simple as asking someone to dinner.

Discussion Questions:

(1) Where is Jesus asking you to heal history? This is the same question as the last one in the previous chapter. It's so important, it's worth repeating. If you are a redeemed child of God, then the healing of history is part of your calling — so if you don't know the answer to this question, ask the Holy Spirit.

(2) Do you think Cleopas and Mary were aware they were part of the healing of history as they walked the Emmaus road? So, do we need to know all the details of what to do and where to go?

(3) Jesus appointed Mary Magdalene as His 'watchtower' — the meaning of Magdalene — and thereby a repository of memory. He effectively gave to his aunt Mary and her husband, Cleopas, an office as interpreters of prophecy. They had the Jesus-sanctioned insider view on how the Scriptures pertained to His life, death and resurrection. Despite the hiddenness of these women, what does this say about the value Jesus accorded them?

(4) Emmaus was the site of two great military victories against foreign overlords. How did Jesus, by his actions, show that the 'war messiah' was very different from the common expectation?

(5) The return of the vice-regency of earth to the company of believers means we are called to 'keep' the earth well. What can you do to be a better steward?

(6) At the end of this story, the narrator says she's never seen an angel but is consoled because she's seen the Messiah. Yet many of us do not have that comfort — we have never seen Jesus in the flesh. So, how do you respond to the words of Jesus to Thomas as his doubts were swept away: '*Because you have seen Me, you have believed; blessed are those who have not seen and yet have believed*'? (John 20:29)

Prayer:

Father, You are always ready to work with us to heal the bentness and brokenness of our nation. However we are a bent and broken people and You wait on us until we recognise and confess our own bentness and brokenness.

We need to recognise that You are the centre of the universe, not us. We need to repent, to forgive, to accept forgiveness and to align our heart with the heart of Jesus so that we can stand straight and whole.

Today, when we hear Your call may we recognise it as a call to *yasher* — a call to all that is straight and whole. A call to all that is good, upright, pleasant and prosperous. A call to personal healing. A call to heal relationships. A call to heal our nation. A call to partner with You to turn ourselves and our nation right way up.

Father, I admit that I am bent, broken and powerless. Today, I come before You in the power of the Holy Spirit and in the name of Your Son Jesus and confess my pride. At times, I am even proud of my humility. I want to do things my way. I even want You to do things my way. The prayer of my lips is so often different from the prayer of my heart. 'Not Your will but mine be done, Lord,' is my secret plea.

Lord God, I repent. I am sorry. Heal me, please. Cleanse me and make me a vessel fit for the Master's use.

Father, I want to partner with You to turn this world right way up. Father, begin with me. Clear away my doubts, sweep aside my expectations, blow up my excuses and make my heart burn with understanding of who You are. Cause my heart to sing with fire and show me how You want me to share Your story with others. Talk to me on the journey, walk with me on the journey.

In Jesus' beloved name,

Amen

Acknowledgments & Attributions

Photo and Arts Credits

Cover – Volodymyr Burdyak/ Creative Market | Description: Deer on Meadow in Summer; ysbrandcosijn/istockphoto | Description: Roe deer doe on misty forest trail at dawn

Page 7 – McIninch/ CanStockPhoto | Description: Entrance to the Tomb

Page 8 – Romolo Tavani/ Dreamstime.com | Description: Crucifixion At Sunrise – Empty Tomb With Shroud – Resurrection Of Jesus Christ

Page 10 – Glenda Powers/ Dreamstime.com | Description: Outside the Garden Tomb (replica) in which Jesus was buried and rose.

Page 11 – Anneke Schram/ Dreamstime.com | Description: Mary Magdalene crying at the tomb

Page 12 – Beckon Creative; CanStockPhoto | Descriptions: china style textures and backgrounds with space for text or image, asia style textures and backgrounds; feather graphcis by Natalka Dmitrova | Creative Market

Page 14 – Bernard Dunne/ Dreamstime.com | Jesus and sunset

Page 15 – Beckon Creative; iloveotto/ CanStockPhoto | Description: Chinese style texture and background

Page 16 – Pearl/ Lightstock | Description: Mary Magdalene at the tomb

Page 17 – Rick Short/ Lightstock | Description: Woman with donkey

Page 18 – Gino Santa Maria/ Dreamstime.com | Description: Roman Soldier Surprised by an Angel

Page 19 – Metropolitan Museum of Art | Description: Resheph (Public Domain)

Page 21 – Romolo Tavani/ Dreamstime.com | Description: Crucifixion and Resurrection of Jesus – Empty Tomb

Page 22 – Genevieve Arthy | Description: Mary Magdalene weeps for Jesus

Page 24/25 – burgasov/ istockphoto | Description: Pomegranate stock photo

Page 27 – lanasphotos/ istockphoto | Description: Blooming pomegranate tree with small red fruits and flowers

Page 28/29 – Rick Schroeppel/ Lightstock | Description: The Empty Tomb

Page 31 – lermannika/ CanStockPhoto | Description: Flowering tree in an historic place

Page 32 – javax/CanStockPhoto | Description: Sebastia, ancient Israeli excavation

Page 34 – lermannika/ CanStockPhoto | Description: Old almond tree

Page 35 – Beckon Creative; CanStockPhoto | Descriptions: asia style textures and backgrounds

Page 36 – Olga/ istockphoto | Description: Beautiful serious girl with a headscarf

Page 37 – Pearl/ Lightstock | Description: Mary will bear a child

Page 38 – Donna Ho | Description: The Gate at Emmaus

Page 39 – Kristina Linton/ istockphoto | Description: Collect your manna

Page 41 – Journey Box Media/ Lightstock | Description: Jesus in the manger

Page 43 – Annelyier / Dreamstime.com | Description: Blooming Manna Ash

Page 44 – Tashaka2000/ CanStockPhoto | Description: A bottle of myrrh on slate background

Page 46 – LUMO – The Gospels for the Visual Age/ Lightstock | Description: Jesus and disciples

Page 47 – Pearl/ Lightstock | Description: Jesus is crucified

Page 49 – Honourableandbold/ Dreamstime.com | Description: Red deer stag in lush green growth foggy forest

Page 50 – Pearl/ Lightstock | Description: Peter, John and Mary at the tomb

Page 51 – Geoffrey Price/ Unsplash | Description: Brown and gray deer

Page 52/53 – Ampersandmiami/Dreamstime.com | Description: Seder plate used to celebrate the Jewish Passover

Page 55 – denisgo/ CanStockPhoto | Description: Jewish celebrate Pesach with eggs

Page 56 – Windward Images/ Lightstock | Description: Prepare for battle

Page 59 – Kristina Linton/ istockphoto | Description: Israelite woman gathering manna

Page 60 – Antonio Gravante/ Lightstock | Description: Jesus breaks bread

Page 61 – photovs/ CanStockPhoto | Description: Passover food Pesach candlesticks with lit candles

Page 63 – Genevieve Arthy | Description: The Road to Emmaus

Page 64/65 – Feather graphcis by Natalka Dmitrova | Creative Market

Page 67 – Joris Beugels/ Unsplash | Description: Moose running on body of water near mountains during daytime

Design, including endpapers and floral iconography: Beckon Creative | beckoncreative.biz

Deer icons by Carrie Stephens, Bakara and Viktoria.1703

Poem on page 1: *Deer at the Red Sea* from *In the Chariot of Fire*,© Abraham Sutzkever 1945.
   Reprinted by permission of University of California Press

Bible Versions

Scripture quotations used in colour (red or blue) throughout the text are taken from the Holy Bible, New International Version®, NIV®. Copyright © 1973, 1978, 1984, 2011 by Biblica, Inc.™ Used by permission of Zondervan. All rights reserved worldwide. www.zondervan.com The "NIV" and "New International Version" are trademarks registered in the United States Patent and Trademark Office by Biblica, Inc™.

Scripture quotations marked BSB are taken from the The Holy Bible, Berean Study Bible, BSB Copyright ©2016 by Bible Hub Used by Permission. All Rights Reserved Worldwide.

Scripture quotations marked CJB are taken from the Complete Jewish Bible by David H. Stern. Copyright © 1998. All rights reserved. Used by permission of Messianic Jewish Publishers, 6120

Scripture quotations marked ESV are taken from the ESV® Bible (The Holy Bible, English Standard Version®), copyright © 2001 by Crossway, a publishing ministry of Good News Publishers. Used by permission. All rights reserved.

Scripture quotations marked GNT are from the Good News Translation in Today's English Version- Second Edition Copyright © 1992 by American Bible Society. Used by Permission.

Scripture quotations marked HCSB®, are taken from the Holman Christian Standard Bible®, Copyright © 1999, 2000, 2002, 2003, 2009 by Holman Bible Publishers. Used by permission. HCSB® is a federally registered trademark of Holman Bible Publishers.

Scripture quotations marked LEB are taken from the *Lexham English Bible*. Copyright 2012 Logos Bible Software. Lexham is a registered trademark of Logos Bible Software.

Scripture quotations marked NAS are taken from the New American Standard Bible®, Copyright © 1960, 1962, 1963, 1968, 1971, 1972, 1973, 1975, 1977, 1995 by The Lockman Foundation. Used by permission. (www.Lockman.org)

© Anne Hamilton 2020

Published by Armour Books

P. O. Box 492, Corinda QLD 4075 AUSTRALIA

ISBN: 9781925380248

All rights reserved. No part of this publication may be reproduced, stored in, or introduced into a retrieval system, or transmitted, in any form, or by any means (electronic, mechanical, photocopying, recording or otherwise) without the prior written permission of the publisher.

A catalogue record for this book is available from the National Library of Australia

Love's redeeming work is done;
fought the fight, the battle won:
lo, our Sun's eclipse is o'er,
lo, he sets in blood no more.

Vain the stone, the watch, the seal;
Christ has burst the gates of hell;
death in vain forbids his rise;
Christ has opened paradise.

Lives again our glorious King;
where, O death, is now thy sting?
dying once, he all doth save;
where thy victory, O grave?

Soar we now where Christ has led,
following our exalted Head;
made like him, like him we rise;
ours the cross, the grave, the skies.

Charles Wesley

www.ingramcontent.com/pod-product-compliance
Lightning Source LLC
Chambersburg PA
CBHW050759110526
44588CB00002B/56